T0128012

.

God's Ordained
Life *in a*
Nutshell,
never too late

MAE WARTELL

WESTBOW
PRESS®
A DIVISION OF THOMAS NELSON
& ZONDERVAN

WestBow Press books may be ordered through booksellers or by contacting:

WestBow Press
A Division of Thomas Nelson & Zondervan
1663 Liberty Drive
Bloomington, IN 47403
www.westbowpress.com
1 (866) 928-1240

ISBN: 978-1-5127-5600-5 (sc)

Print information available on the last page.

WestBow Press rev. date: 11/04/2016

DEDICATION

I dedicate this book to Jesus Christ, Lord of my life! He is the one who inspired me to write this book on Friday morning, November 20, 2015. That is the day that he planted the idea in my heart. Is there anything too hard for God? The answer is no! All power is in his hands and through him all things are possible.

God's Book

God's Purpose

God's Plan

To God be the Glory, Honor, and the Praise
He is Worthy!

"And when I am lifted up from the earth,
I will draw everyone to myself (John 12:32)."

ACKNOWLEDGMENTS

I would like to thank my mother, Evelyn Newman, for all the prayers sent up while composing this book. Also, thanks go out to my son Michael, his spouse Monique, and my grandkids: Micah, Jillian, Ramir, Mykayla, Maryanna, Kaliyah, and My'Lanna, who have all proven to be an inspiration and a great source of encouragement. My hope is that this book will serve as a legacy for all my grandkids now and to come so that they will discover God's path to life.

Secondly, I would like to thank Nicola Lessig, from Aids Foundation Houston where I currently volunteer, for her help and support with the technical issues.

Finally, I cannot end without giving thanks to others who contributed in any way, and to everyone who reads this book and shares the good news.

I thank you all from the bottom of my heart!

CONTENTS

FOREWORD

My daughter, Mae Wartell, is a devout Christian who was called to full-time Missionary service in January 2015. She is a faithful member of Champion Forest Baptist Church since 2003 and currently under the leadership of Dr. David Fleming. Mae has worked as a Registered Nurse for many years. She was inspired by the Holy Spirit to write this book entitled <u>God's Ordained Life in a Nutshell, never too late</u>. I believe that this book will touch many lives and bring Glory to God.

Your loving mother
Evelyn Newman

INTRODUCTION

My name is Mae Wartell, a nurse by profession, called by God to serve as a full-time missionary and inspired by him to write this book. The intent of this book, as revealed by the Holy Spirit, is to provide a simple path to discovering God's destiny for the lives of his children. It is fairly easy to choose between good and bad, but what about choosing between good and best? This scenario is a bit more challenging, but the best plan is always God's choice. His plan affords us the opportunity to experience joy, the unspeakable joy that the bible teaches about, and to fulfill our God-given purpose here on Earth. The bible speaks about two paths in life; God's way or the way of the world. There are also two paths in the life of a Christian; the satisfied risk-free life that assures us of going to heaven, or the leap of faith life that drives us into God's best.

Which will you choose?

This book is a blueprint of God's best life, and it reminds me of the little boy with two fish and 5 loaves of bread that God multiplied and fed 5,000 people. I believe that God will take this book and do the same; even more.

> "The Lord answered; if you have faith even as small as a mustard seed, you can say to this mountain, move from here to there, and it will move. Nothing will be impossible for you (Matthew 17:20)."

1

The Walk

OBEDIENCE

"Therefore, since we are surrounded by such a huge crowd of witnesses to the life of faith, let us strip off every weight that slows us down, especially the sin that so easily trips us up. And let us run with endurance the race God set before us. We do this by keeping our eyes on Jesus, the champion who initiates and perfects our faith (Hebrews 12:2)."

A New Life

"Therefore, if anyone is in Christ, the new creation has come,
the old is gone, the new is here (2 Corinthians 5:17, NIV)."

Many a new believer imagine the Christian Life as easy and almost carefree with God as Captain of the ship. When we are saved, we experience unspeakable joy; an earmark in the life of a Christian. We cannot get enough of God's word, and our brain becomes sponge-like; soaking up every bit of wisdom that we can. It is very exciting to witness and share God's word. We are pleased and thankful that God has chosen us to live with him in eternity.

Spiritual Growth

Then God expects us to grow. We start off as babies in Christ.

"Like newborn babies, crave pure spiritual milk, so that by
it you may grow up in your salvation (1 Peter 2:2)."

God takes us by our hand, and he leads us one step at a time. Then he begins to give us a little more, and a little more responsibility as we begin to mature, and so the testing of our faith begins.

HARD WORK

The Christian life involves hard work. We must be willing to surrender anything that endangers our relationship with God. We must run with endurance and struggle against sin, drawing upon the power of the Holy Spirit. To live effectively, we must keep our eyes on Jesus. We will stumble if we look away from him to stare at ourselves, or at the circumstances surrounding us. He is The Author and Perfecter of our faith. We should live for Christ, not self. He must occupy center stage in our lives. **Keep God First!**

THE CALL TO OBEDIENCE

God has called us to a life of obedience. He is a God of purpose and has a reason for all that he does. He promises in Romans 8:28, "And we know that God causes all things to work together for the good of those who love God and are called according to his purpose for them." Obedience opens the communication channels between us and God, while disobedience closes those channels. It secures the fellowship connection and allows God to instruct and guide us in the way we should go. God promises to guide us into our destiny with love and wisdom if we allow him. "For I the Lord will speak, and whatever word I speak will be performed (Ezekiel 12:25)." God warns us that we should not be stubborn and have to be controlled by discipline and punishment. Because God is a loving and faithful God, he will do his part if we do ours. Obedience allows God to bless us and show us his way of life. It is our road to success, according to God's standards. Also, it is our path to fulfillment, love, and kindness toward us. A life of obedience opens the door that allows God to fulfill his ultimate purpose through us. His purpose in all things is to bring Glory to himself and to use us to be a blessing to others. There is no greater joy. Make that commitment to be obedient to God, and he will reward you with blessings that only he can give: love, peace, joy, security, and prosperity to name a few. You will experience God's favor, and in return give him all the Glory that he deserves.

> "For we are God's masterpiece. He has created us anew in Christ Jesus, so we can do the good things he planned for us long ago (Ephesians 2:1)."

PRAYER FOR OBEDIENCE

Heavenly Father, I ask that you would stir and give increase to a burning desire in my heart, that I may walk in obedience to your will, one day at a time; always aware that you are in control. I ask that you provide strength, wisdom, and discernment for the journey. Please help me to be vigilant and always aware that our adversary, Satan, is on the prowl. He seeks whom he can devour, and he comes to kill my joy, steal my hope, and reek havoc in my life and also in the lives of those I love. When the road gets rough, please help me to remember that you never said it would be easy, but you have promised never to forsake me. Remind me that the battle is not mine; it belongs to you. I know that I have the victory through the blood of Jesus that was shed on the Cross for my sins. I am more than a conqueror through Jesus Christ who loves me. Amen

2
The Requirement

COMPLETE SURRENDER

"So I say walk by the Spirit, and you will not gratify the desires of the flesh. For the flesh desires what is contrary to the Spirit, and the Spirit what is contrary to the flesh. They are in conflict with each other, so that you are not to do whatever you want (Galatians 5:16-17, NIV)."

GOD'S SACRIFICE

Jesus Christ paid the ultimate sacrifice when he died on the Cross for our sins. That sacrifice gave us access to eternal life. From noon until three in the afternoon darkness came over all the land. About three in the afternoon Jesus cried out in a loud voice, " Eli, Eli, lema sabachthani?(which means My God, my God, why have you forsaken me?) Then

Jesus shouted out again and released his Spirit (Matthew 27:45-46-50, NIV)."

God's sacrifice was a deep expression of his love for mankind, Agape Love, which is the highest form of love. Abraham is a great example of love and devotion to Christ. His willingness to sacrifice Isaac, his only son, in obedience to God's command is unprecedented and defies human nature. God tested Abraham to his tipping point when he raised his knife to murder Isaac. He intervened and provided a ram in the bush. Through it all, Abraham continued to trust that the promise God had made of life, hope, and a future would come to pass, not only for him but also for his heirs, even if God had to raise Isaac from the dead. Abraham was a great example for us all. **He totally surrendered!**

OUR SACRIFICE

God calls us to a life of sacrifice and total surrender to his will. He wants us to take one day at a time trusting that his will is the best place to be, and knowing that all power is in his hands. He is the Alpha and Omega; the beginning and the end. He is the King of Glory: omnipotent, omnipresent, and omniscient. There is nothing our God can't do. He is the creator of Heaven and Earth.

Then Jesus said to the disciples; "If any of you wants to be my follower, you must turn from your selfish ways, take up your cross, and follow me. If you try to hang on to your life, you will loose it, but if you give up your life for my sake, you will save it (Matthew 16: 24-25)."

WHAT DOES IT MEAN TO SACRIFICE?

A sacrifice is an act of an offering to God. It is something precious. Also, it is destruction or surrender of something for the sake of something else. When Jesus used the picture of his followers taking up their crosses to follow him, the Disciples knew what he meant. Crucifixion was a common Roman method of execution and condemned criminals had to carry their cross through the streets to the execution site. Following Jesus, therefore, meant a true commitment, the risk of death, and no turning back. The possibility of losing their lives was very real for the Disciples and also for Jesus. Real discipleship implies real commitment. If we protect ourselves from the pain that God calls us to suffer, we will begin to die spiritually and emotionally. Our lives will turn inward, and we will loose our intended purpose of living. Sacrifice is an expression of our deep love and devotion toward God. Sometimes the sacrifice may be a job, relationship, finances, etc. Whatever God has to remove from our lives to teach us total reliance on him, he will. Not because he is a mean and selfish God, but because he is a loving and caring God who wants the best for us. Total reliance on him is a necessary step on our journey to fulfilling God's purpose for our lives, the abundant life. Total surrender is not an easy task. It is the result of growth, and maturity through our relationship with the Lord, which we accomplish through prayer, meditation, reading God's word, hearing it taught, fellowship, etc. These activities fuel our desire for the Lord, give us strength, build our faith, and enable us to surrender our lives to Christ. Then we learn to put him first in our lives; his rightful place. Self will go kicking and screaming, but self has got to go! This act of courage, along with the others mentioned previously, will place you in the center of God's will. There you will realize that his way is perfect and that there is no place on earth that you would rather be. This will be the start of a new beginning to the Yellow Brick Road that leads to God's purpose for your life.

> "For I know the plans I have for you, declares the Lord, plans to prosper you and not to harm you, plans to give you hope and a future (Jeremiah 29:11)."

GOD IS OUR SOURCE AND OUR SECURITY.

> "I am the vine; you are the branches. If you remain in me, and I in you, you will bear much fruit; apart from me, you can do nothing (John 15:5)."

We are God's witnesses to the lost and a testament to his goodness and power. An example to the world and an opportunity for the lost to come to Christ and receive everlasting life. Whenever God calls us to sacrifice, he rewards us with a blessing, and he has a purpose for it. Surrender of our will is a matter of trust.

SERVICE

GIVING OF OURSELVES TO THE LORD

Service is an important component of sacrifice. Jesus requires our commitment. He expects us to pledge our whole existence to him. "Commit to the Lord whatever you do, and your plans will succeed (Prov 16:3)." This means trusting God as if everything depends on him while working as if everything depends on us. Our jobs should be viewed as a place of service to the Lord. God says, "Work with enthusiasm, as though you were working for the Lord rather than for people (Ephesians 6:7)." "For even the son of man came not to be served, but to serve others and to give his life as a ransom for many (Mark 10:25)."

We don't have to look far to discover places to serve. We encounter opportunities everywhere we go. Many people today need help. There are also many opportunities to serve in the church. Make that commitment today, and you will please God, and also get one step closer to fulfilling his purpose in your life.

MOTIVE BEHIND OUR ACTIONS

God looks at our motives or the reasons behind our actions. He desires that our motives are pure, originating from a place of love, not a place of self-gain.(Proverbs 16:2) says, "All a person's ways seem pure to them, but motives are weighed by the Lord." (Jeremiah 17:9) says, "The human heart is deceitful above all things and beyond cure. Who can understand it?"

We can easily fool ourselves about our own motives. We can pretend that we are choosing certain actions for God, or the benefit of others, when in reality we have selfish reasons. God is not fooled by our selfishness and he knows the thoughts and intents of our heart. Human Beings can operate from a variety of motivations, often negative: pride, anger, revenge, a sense of entitlement, or the desire for approval can all be catalysts for our actions.* Any motivation that originates in our sinful flesh is not pleasing to God. (Romans 8:8) *God even evaluates the condition of our hearts when we give offerings to him. (2 Corinthians 9:7) *Selfish motives can hinder our prayers. "When you ask you do not receive, because you ask with wrong motives, that you may spend what you get on your pleasures (James 4:3, NIV)." Because our hearts are so deceitful, we should constantly evaluate our own motives and be honest with ourselves about why we are choosing a certain action.

SO WHAT IS THE RIGHT MOTIVATION?

(1 Thessalonians 2:4, NIV) says that our purpose is to please God not people. He alone examines the motives of our hearts. God is interested in our motives even more than our actions. (1 Corinthians 4:5, NIV) says that when Jesus comes again, he will bring to light what is hidden in darkness, and will reveal our private motives. At that time each will

receive their due praise from God. God wants us to know that he sees what no one else sees. He knows why we do what we do, and desires to reward those whose hearts are right toward him. We can keep our motives pure by continually surrendering every part of our hearts to the control of the Holy Spirit. Motivation becomes an issue when we are not honest with ourselves about why we are doing things. When we give the outward appearance of obeying God, but our hearts are hard, God knows. We are deceiving ourselves and others also. The only way we can operate from pure motives is when we allow the Holy Spirit to guide our lives. Then we will walk in the Spirit and not gratify the desires of the flesh. (Galatians 5:16, NIV) When we allow God to control every part of us, then our desire is to please him and not ourselves. Our flesh constantly clamors to exalt itself, and only when we walk in the Spirit will we not gratify those desires. David is our example as he asks the Lord in Psalms 51, "Create in me a clean heart, O God. Renew the stain of my guilt." Because we are born sinners, our natural inclination is to please ourselves rather than God. Like David we must ask God to cleanse us from within, filling our hearts and spirits with new thoughts and desires. Right conduct can come only from a clean heart and spirit. Ask God to create a pure heart and spirit in you.

Here are some specific questions to help us evaluate our own motives.

1. If no one ever knows what I am doing, giving, serving, sacrificing, would I still do it?

2. If there was no visible payoff for doing this, would I still do it?

3. Would I joyfully take a lesser position if God asked me to?

4. Am I doing this for the praise of others or how it makes me feel?

5. If I had to suffer for continuing what God has called me to do, would I continue?

6. If others misunderstand or criticize my actions, would I stop?

7. If those whom I am serving never show gratitude or repay me in any way will I still do it?

8. Do I judge my success or failure based upon my faithfulness to what God has asked me to do, or how I compare to others?

PRAYER OF SACRIFICE

Lord, I come into your presence with an open heart, asking that you create in me a clean heart so that I can serve you in **Spirit and Truth.** Your word says that you are truth, so I ask that you empower me to live a life that honors you. I know that giving of myself to others is a way of glorifying you, so I ask that you shower my heart with compassion and love, allowing that love to radiate into the heart of everyone I meet. Lord, you are my compass, please guide and direct me to the place of service that you know is a perfect fit for the life that you have planned for me in advance. Help me to be that beacon of light that shines into the lives of others and plants seeds into their hearts, so they may gain an awareness of your goodness, mercy, and power. Help me to surrender my life to you daily, stripping off the old and adorning with the new, so that I may walk in the spirit while denying the flesh. You are God Almighty who sheds your love on us all, no respecter of persons. You deserve all the Glory and all the praise. In Jesus name, I pray, Amen!

3
The Foundation

FAITH

"Faith is the confidence that what we hope for will actually happen; It gives us assurance about things we cannot see (Hebrews 11:1)."

THE ESSENCE OF FAITH

The beginning point of faith is believing in God's character; he is who he says he is. The endpoint is believing in God's promises; he will do what he says he will do. When we believe that God will fulfill his promises even though we don't see the promises materializing yet, we demonstrate faith.

"So do not throw away this confident trust in the Lord. Remember the great reward it brings you. Patient endurance is what you need now, so that you will continue to do God's will. Then you will receive all that he has promised. For in just a little while the coming one will come and not delay, and my righteous ones will live by faith. But I will take no pleasure in anyone who turns away (Hebrews 10:35-38)."

Faith Demonstrated

David was a man of great faith, who was trained through the experience of fighting off dangerous animals while working as a sheepherder. His skills and confidence were perfected. He trusted God to see him through each challenge and he came out on top. He exercised belief and trust while continuing to grow to the culmination of defeating Goliath with a rock and a slingshot.

The bible gives us a clear choice between two contrasting pathways in life. As Christians, we are expected to take the higher road even though it looks more arduous and bumpy. It is also mysterious. It gets steep in places and the climb takes a toll on our energy. It gets lonely, not many people on it, but more than you might imagine, and some because of your example. It gets slippery, as Satan blows ice on the narrow passages. But despite its perceived dangers, the higher road is bound for the peak, and you will make it if you don't give up. God has a lifeline around you. Whenever you are tempted to falter in your faith or to turn back from following Christ, just remember to stay focused on what God has done for you, and what he offers in the future. Then look up and say a prayer, but keep climbing. The Lord is always in your circumstances with you as he was with the three Hebrew boys, Shadrach, Meshach, and Abednego in Daniel chapter 3.

The road of faith has been a rocky one for me. I was born again in 1988. God rescued me from the pit of Hell, that Satan tried so desperately to secure as my future home but failed. Only through Christ do I now have the victory. I veered off the path, practiced disobedience, and tenaciously held on to my will even as a Christian, but God has brought me to a place in my life where I can honestly say; not my will but Thine will be done. I have learned the significance of obedience to God after much trial and much error. I still experience moments of weakness when Satan attempts to confuse me, tempt me and tries to make me doubt God, but God rescues me every time with his word; the sword of the spirit. The Holy Spirit then illuminates my mind and reveals the perpetrator as Satan, the master deceiver. God never forsakes us. I remember when I purchased my home. The builder and I had a conflict. I wanted repairs made in advance, but he wanted to delay until after closing, so he sold the home to a second buyer. I was dumbfounded because I was sure God had led me to purchase this particular home. Then one day while at my mom's home God spoke loud and clear. He said, are you going to believe what you see or what I said? I took a stand and bought the home and God worked everything out. I live in the home to this day, and God has blessed me to pay off a thirty-year mortgage in twelve years. This is another example of God's faithfulness. He always comes through according to his will, but we have to trust him. We have to walk by faith and not by sight. God is our continuous help in the time of trouble. (Hebrews 11:6, NIV) says, "Without faith it is impossible to please God. Anyone who wants to come to him must believe that God exists and that he rewards those who sincerely seek him."

The Christian journey is not traveled alone. God is always present to provide and encourage us along the way. He provides manna from Heaven; nourishment for whatever ails us. In my life, God has used visions as a primary source of communication to assist in keeping me on track. A vision is a miraculous revelation of God's truth. A glimpse into the future of what is to come. These visions have given me hope, and the encouragement needed to continue on the path. God's word is true. (Isaiah 55:11, NIV) says, "So will my word be which goes forth from my mouth; It will not return to me empty, without accomplishing what I desire, and without succeeding in the matter for which I sent it." To be honest, in addition to the visions God has also used discipline. I am somewhat of a slow learner. The most difficult lesson for me as for probably the majority of us has been total surrender to God: mind, body, and soul. I would always think that I had totally surrendered only to realize later that I had not. I would surrender 90% while attempting to conceal 10% in the corner of my heart, but guess what, God found it and exposed me. It took time because I held on for dear life always hoping that my hiding place would go unnoticed; absurd huh? I never seemed to remember that word omniscient.

I am a nurse by profession and have been single most of my life. I just have never met the right guy; God's choice. My means of survival has always been my Nursing License. God has chipped away at this ability through the years in order to claim his rightful place on the throne of my heart. He has created adversities that stripped me of my paychecks, leaving me with little to no income, but he always comes through. He has always provided far more than I could ever ask or hope, while simultaneously grooming and developing my faith; all the while molding and shaping me into the new creature that he predestined me to become. I have learned to rely on God with or without a job, one day at a time, trusting him as my provider. His goal is to grow us to a point in our lives so that he can open the door to our destiny. I have learned that his will is the best place to be. It's the place where God takes care of us and takes responsibility for any consequences. He is a powerful God, and he is our creator; the master of Heaven and Earth. He gave us life and desires that we freely surrender that life back to him. This step of Faith will open the door to God's Abundant Life. Hallelujah!

Preparation

God prepares us before he leads us to our destiny. Adversity is a tool that he chooses to use. He stretches our faith in order to strengthen and build our character. God refines us so that we may become useful for his glory. (James 2:26) says, "Faith without works is dead." Living a life of service to others is pleasing to God. We are all encouraged by a leader who stirs us to move forward; someone who believes in us and will be there to support us in any tasks that may come our way. God is that kind of leader. He is working in us to light a fire of desire and power that will motivate us to do that which will give him glory and praise.

As long as God, who controls our future, provides our agenda and goes with us as we fulfill his mission, we can be successful God's way. The bible states that "No weapon forged against us will prevail (Isaiah 54:17, NIV)." This is our heritage and vindication from our Lord, so armor up and march in the army of the Lord. This is not a blank check that will guarantee freedom from pain, suffering, or hardship because these are useful tools in God's hands. Although, we do have God's assurance that he will see us through to a glorious conclusion. Many times God will target our weaknesses to cleanse and build our faith. Think of cleaning out a closet. God is meticulous and includes every nook and cranny in his cleaning process. Remember that word omniscient? Cleansing is a good thing and makes us useful for God's work.

I spent many years in the preparation season of my life. Satan corrupted my mind with self-destructive thoughts, bad behaviors, misconceptions, and pride. I was in bondage to my independent nature and my self-will and needed to be stripped; sound familiar? Many times what we perceive as good is only good in our own eyes; God may have a different perspective. As a result of my twisted mindset, God placed me in situations with my back up against a wall and all I could do was look up. He stripped away all my safety nets including my lively hood. Then he revealed that he wanted me to go out on a limb for him; no safety net. My knees began to shake, and I found myself at a crossroad or crisis of belief. Suddenly, I was faced with the most difficult choice of my life; follow God or turn back. I did not even have a clue as to where I was headed. All I knew was that I did not like the sound of going out on a limb. I felt like turning around and just running away screaming; but I thought, I have come too far to turn around, and so I decided to step out on faith. God took me into a period of intense spiritual development and taught me that he is my sole provider, and also in control of my life. I had to weather the storm. God is who he says he is and will do what he says. He holds the key to all things. Almighty God possesses the power to open any door, but he also has the power to keep it shut. It has been a struggle, but God has been faithful through it all. He provides his way, and in his time. His timing may not always line up with the bill collectors timing, but he is always on time; just in the nick of time. He marches to his own drumbeat, but never fails to deliver. What an awesome God we serve! "For my thoughts are not your thoughts, neither are your ways my ways, declares the Lord. As the heavens are higher than the earth, so are my ways higher than your ways and my thoughts than your thoughts (Isaiah 55: 8-9, NIV)." Our Savior has a purpose for everything he does.

My boot camp training has prepared me to witness to the less fortunate through the trials of experience. (2 Corinthians 1:3-4) says, "God is our merciful Father and the source of all comfort. He comforts us in all our troubles so that we can comfort others. When they are troubled, we will be able to give them the same comfort God has given us." This journey has been very adventurous with its ups and downs, twists and turns, highways and byways, but actually, it is a blessing when you look back because the things you learn are priceless. You enter the boot camp as an oyster, but you emerge as a pearl. Also, on the flip side of the trial are great blessings and the privilege to serve in the perfect plan that God created just for you. We are all unique and intricately woven by the designer himself. He is awesome and when praises go up he sends blessings down. I tell you he replied, "If they keep quiet the stones will cry out (Luke:19:40, NIV)." God's plan is perfected for each life. His ways always seem to amaze me. Some know him as the <u>Lily of the Valley the Bright and Morning Star.</u> Who is this God, also known as Jesus, who died on the Cross for our sins, so that all may have access to eternal life? He is the God of Jacob and Abraham, Paul and Silas, David and Joseph. He is our God, and he reigns supreme, pouring out his spirit into us. He teaches, grows, and sanctifies us, so that we may mature and become more like him.

In my weakest moment, God gave me a vision. Whenever I would visualize my struggle, I would see the image of God dangling above it, and my eyes would immediately be drawn to his image hovering over my problem. Suddenly, I would feel safe and at peace. The Holy Spirit revealed this as perfect faith; seeing and trusting God above any difficulty, and feeling safe and at peace; knowing that he will work everything out for my good and for his Glory, and I would be ok. If only I could stay there permanently, in perfect peace. Suddenly, it became clear to me that this revelation of perfect peace equips a Christian, in a dire situation, to remain calm, peaceful, and faithful to God. (Philippians: 4:6) Deliverance from the situation should not be our primary focus. Our primary focus should be remaining faithful to God, even if he decides not to rescue us, but instead to comfort and guide us through our circumstances. He already knows how we will respond; but do we? God has brought me to this particular place in my life, so that when I step into my destiny as an ordained Missionary,

I will be able to stand and not collapse: by drawing on his strength, following his lead, and keeping that relationship connection. So my point to all of this is to encourage you to endure the preparation phase and surrender all to God's will. It has been tailor-made for you so that you will be equipped for your God ordained destiny. God does equip whomever he calls. "May he equip you with all you need for doing his will (Hebrews 13:21)." This too shall pass, and you will come out on the other side ready to be used by God. He will transition you into **God's Ordained Life.** This is a utopia and the best place to be, God's will. It is the place where you can impact lives for Christ, and experience the joy of giving to others on a magnified scale; the place where blessings flow. Remember, God never said it would be easy, but it will be very much worth the trouble. God will bring you through, in due time. His spiritual timing is understood only by him. He is our wonderful Counselor and Prince of Peace. He is God! Let everything that hath breath Praise the Lord! Weeping may endure for a night, but joy comes in the morning when our hope is in God.

Jesus is our prime example. He overcame satanic attacks in the wilderness and defeated Satan with the word of God. (Luke 41:1-11) We should follow his example. Words of wisdom from the past have anchored and assisted me on my quest to discovering my God ordained destiny. Those words have served as a source of strength and encouragement, affording me the sustenance to stay the course. I have learned to release, relax, and rely, putting all in God's hands.

When I look back I realize that God has been grooming me for this mission for many many years. Sometimes he places desires in our hearts and we are totally unaware of his activity. He also leads and guides us by that same method at times.

In March 2015, while at the gym, God revealed that me and a partner are destined to embark upon a special mission. The mission was described as a Crusade for people with Aids. This was stunning to me. I kept playing the words over and over in my head trying to make sense of it all. Once I arrived at my vehicle, God revealed a vision of me and that same partner on a plane to an unknown destination. Remember that a vision is a glimpse into the future of something to come. I discerned that the plane was traveling overseas to a distant land. The events remained foggy in my head until days later while standing in the kitchen, when suddenly a light flashed through my mind. At that moment, I suddenly understood that the vision depicted a calling on my life, to become a full-time Missionary ordained by God. This took me aback, because never in a million years would I have ever had even an inkling of becoming a full-time ordained Missionary; especially at this time in my life when I pictured myself retiring in a few years, serving locally, and visiting some of those places I have seen on Diners, Drive-ins, and Dives. My emotions were mixed and vacillated. I wasn't quite sure whether to be happy, sad, or fearful. As God revealed more and more, I started to adjust and become more accepting of his plan. You see God does not adjust to us but requires that we adjust to him. I had to submit. Actually, for me, there was no other option. I definitely abhorred the idea of being disobedient, and I did not want to miss God's plan for my life. I have surrendered to his calling and have begun to look forward to my new life to come, and all that it may entail. I have the Holy Spirit's assurance that I won't be alone. God will be with me.

Wherever your God ordained destiny may lead you, this map will help to guide you there.

COMPASS TO DESTINY

OBEDIENCE

proves our devotion to God (1 John 5:2-3)

demonstrates our faithfulness to God (1 John 2:3-6)

glorifies God in the world (1 Peter 2:12)

opens avenues of blessing for us (John 13:17)

TOTAL SURRENDER

"Abraham take your son, your only son, whom you love so much and go to the region of Moriah. Sacrifice him as a burnt offering on one of the mountains which I will show you (Genesis 22:2)."

"And Abraham picked up the knife to kill his son as a sacrifice (Genesis 22:10)"

FAITH

"For we live by faith, not by sight" (2 Corinthians 5:7, NIV)

DESTINY

"I know the plans I have for you, says the Lord. They are plans for good and not for disaster, to give you a future and hope (Jeremiah 29:11, NIV)."

DIRECTIONS IN A NUTSHELL

1. walk in obedience

2. surrender your will

3. live by faith, not by sight

4. discover your destiny

Compass to Endurance

Be Humble (John 15:5)

"Yes, I am the vine; you are the branches. Those who remain in me, and I in them, will produce much fruit"

Keep the Faith (1Kings 8:56)

"Praise the Lord who has given rest to his people Israel, just as he promised. Not one word has failed of all the wonderful promises he gave through his servant Moses."

Be Patient (Isaiah 64:4)

"For since the world began, no ear has heard, and no eye has seen, a God like you, who works for those who wait for him."

Be Courageously Obedient (Josh 1: 7-9)

"Be strong and very courageous. Be careful to obey all the instructions Moses gave you. Do not deviate from them, turning either right or left. Then you will be successful in everything."

Tools to Endure

1. humility

2. faith

3. patience

4. courage

In due time, God will reveal his open door. When he does, trust that he knows what he is doing and follow his lead. His instructions may contrast with human reasoning and there may be fear of the unknown, but if you want more of God's love and power you must be willing to carry out the responsibilities that you are given. We cannot say we truly believe in God if we refuse to obey him. We cannot seek God's love and run from him at the same time. We cannot follow God and stay the same. God is faithful and his word is true.

> "It is the same with my word. I send it out and it always produces fruit. It will accomplish all that I want it to, and it will prosper everywhere I send it (Isaiah 55:11)."

My hope is built on nothing less than Jesus Christ blood and righteousness.

Faith = belief + trust

belief: knowing God's word and what he reveals to you is true

trust: reliance upon God; complete surrender

"Do not be anxious about tomorrow for tomorrow will be anxious for itself: sufficient for the day is its own trouble (Matthew 6:34, NIV)."

God wants us to take one day at a time. Just as God feeds the birds of the air daily, surely he will take care of us.

Be Aware of Satan!

Pay attention to the warning signs!

"Stay alert! Watch out for your great enemy, the devil. He prowls around like a roaring lion, looking for someone to devour (1 Peter 5:8, NIV)."

"The great dragon was hurled down—that ancient serpent called the devil, or Satan, who leads the whole world astray. He was hurled to the earth, and his angels with him (Revelation 12:9, NIV)."

Stop: Danger

"Doubt—Lurking"

**Don't allow doubt to keep you
from reaching your destiny**

**"(James1:6) But when you ask, you must
believe and not doubt, because the one
who doubts is like a wave of the sea,
blown and tossed by the wind."**

Mae Wartell

"Lies—Hidden"

Don't allow Satan's lies to deflect you onto the wrong path

"(Exodus 20:16) You must not testify falsely against your neighbor."

"Fear—Creeping"

Don't allow bumps in the road to deter you

"(Philippians 4:6) Don't worry about anything; instead, pray about everything. Tell God what you need and thank him for all he has done."

"Discouragement"

Don't get sucked into discouragement

"(Joshua 1:9) This is my command-be strong and courageous! Do not be afraid or discouraged. For the Lord your God is with you wherever you go."

"Confusion"

Don't linger in confusion

"(1 Corinthians 14:33) For God is not a God of disorder but of peace, as in all the meetings of God's holy people."

Stop

Think

Observe

Proceed

Hallelujah!

Perfect Faith is when we can envision God above any adversity.

Prayer of Faith

"If we are faithless, he remains faithful, for he cannot deny who he is (2 Timothy 2:13)."

Heavenly Father, you are so faithful, please help me to be faithful to you. Teach me to love you above anything else and to realize that your will is the best place to be. Help me to run this race with endurance, knowing that you are the perfecter of my faith. Father, help me to take one day at a time while keeping my focus on you. You are my source and without you, I can do nothing. You are the Lily of the Valley a bright and morning star whose mercies are anew each day. Lord, your word says that those you call you equip. Help me to stand strong on your promises, the foundation of my life, while putting on the full armor of God each day to thwart the deceptive ploys of Satan launched to destroy your plan for my life. Ingrain your word upon my heart, and help me to understand that I can do all things through Christ who gives me strength. Amen

4

The New Life

ABUNDANT LIFE

This is life in its abounding fullness of joy and strength for mind, body, and soul. It signifies a contrast to feelings of lack, emptiness, and dissatisfaction. Such feelings may motivate a person to seek the meaning of life and a change in their own life.

> "No eye has seen, no ear has heard, and no mind has imagined what God has prepared for those who love him (1Corinthians 2:9)."

Food for Thought!

WHAT IS ABUNDANT LIFE TO YOU?

Is your answer in line with God's word and what he promises?

"For the word of God is alive and powerful. It is sharper than the sharpest two-edged sword, cutting between soul and spirit between joint and marrow. It exposes our innermost thoughts and desires. Nothing in all creation is hidden from God. Everything is naked and exposed before his eyes, and he is the one to whom we are accountable."

(Hebrews 4:12-13)

ABUNDANT LIFE PRAYER

Heavenly Father, I want to thank you for the access to the Abundant Life that you have so graciously made available to me. You are such a loving and gracious God who desires nothing but the best for me. I marvel at your power and your Agape Love toward me. You are the God of Abraham, Paul, and David, and Lord over all. You sacrificed your only son on the cross so that I may have access to everlasting life. Your voice is powerful and majestic. It is sent out and does not return void. Your anger lasts but a moment, but your favor last a lifetime. You work all things together for the good of those who are called according to your purpose. If I had a thousand tongues, I couldn't thank you enough. You deserve all the Glory, the Honor, and the Praise. In the precious name of Jesus, I pray. Amen

MAE WARTELL

5

A Final Word

SERVANT OF CHRIST

This book is a testament to how God can use any of us to accomplish his will. We just need to avail ourselves to him. I am not sure if I will ever write another book. It is not up to me, it is God's decision. My prayer is that this book will give clear direction to God's children, and assist all to walk by faith and not by sight in obedience to God, completely surrendered to his will; so that all may discover God's perfect plan of service for their lives as I have been blessed to do. As we know, prayer allows God to work, not because he is bound by it, but because this is the method God chooses.

> "May the Lord bless and protect you
> May the Lord smile on you and be
> gracious to you. May the Lord show
> you his favor and give you his peace."

(Numbers 6: 24-26)

6

The Outcome

MEMOIR

As I stated earlier, my name is Mae Wartell and the vessel that God has chosen to write this book. The idea was preceded by an illumination from God. Suddenly, before dawn out of nowhere, I was awakened by thoughts of a book title cascading through my mind. I immediately got up and began to write. The information flowed beginning to end, not in one day of course. It took four months to complete; but God! The Holy Spirit revealed and confirmed the title, <u>God's Ordained Life in a Nutshell, never too late.</u>

I have had to resist Satan's tactics, deny thoughts of the flesh, miss meals, and adjust my plans, all in order to complete this book. Even going as far as putting the Young and Restless and Houston Rockets on the shelf; that was hard. Lots of times the Holy Spirit would awaken me at 6:00 am, and I am not an early riser. Frequently, Satan would launch his arrows of doubt, and I would think, no way José, I can't do this and want to quit; but then God would give me a new idea and once I acted on it the information would flow. My personal journey has entailed: bad choices, two bad marriages, mountains and valleys, and lots of discipline. God has never forsaken me, and he has always brought me through. I marvel at his patience because without it I never would have arrived here, destiny, which is the place where I can be used by God to make a difference, and help to bring others to Christ. Our destiny is always about helping others. God never gives up on us and he is always faithful. He only asks that we trust him. Through it all, God kept his hand on me. He is an awesome God. We are the vessels that God uses to plant the seed, but only God can give the increase in the lives of each of his children according to his perfect will.

"I planted the seed in your hearts and Apollos watered it,
    but it was God who made it grow (1Corinthians 3:6)."

God can use us at any age, as long as we have breath in our bodies. He uses us to further his purposes and make significant contributions to his Kingdom if we allow him. We must trust in him and follow his lead. Give God the reigns of your life. He will reward you here on earth and in the afterlife. God has not revealed his intentions for this book, except that it is designed as a simple step method to discovering his will for the lives of his children. I have recognized the open door, and I am stepping out on faith. I trust God, and I have committed my future to him. He has promised to make our enemies our footstool, and I will take that promise wherever I go. I pray that the message of God in this book inspires and assists you to discover your destiny. I am not a bible scholar, nor have I ever written a book, but I have surrendered to the call of God, and the best is yet to come.

TRIBUTE

I have been an avid listener of the teachings of Dr. Charles Stanley for approximately twenty years. He has been an incredible inspiration in my life. Whenever I have lacked the understanding or the knowledge to respond correctly in any given situation, his teaching would provide step by step instructions that even babes in Christ could understand. God has chosen his teachings as a way to speak and grow me over the years, and this encounter has blessed and continues to bless my life today. The principles that he teaches are biblical and when applied correctly they work. They have worked for me over and over again. I have been molded, strengthened, and enlightened by his teachings. They have encouraged me when I have felt like quitting. I have gained wisdom, discernment, learned the ways of God, and so much more. Twenty years ago I saw the connection as a chance encounter, but now I realize it was ordered by God. I recommend his website and devotional at every opportunity.

Thank you, Dr. Stanley, for allowing God to use you for so many years to impact so many lives in a way that inspires Christian growth and unbelievers to seek God.

To God be the glory for the things he has done!

Printed in the United States
By Bookmasters